Cosmos In A Jar

Grace Lalrinpari Hauzel

Published by Gumby Publishers, 2023.

Published by Gumby Publishers,
36 Saint John's Place
Freeport 11520-4618
New York, USA

Airhub 1425, UBX 6 Poyle Trading Estate,
Colndale Road, Colnbrook
Slough SL30AA
Berkshire, United Kingdom

Table of Contents

About The Author

Grace Lalrinpari Hauzel is an enthusiastic budding writer who has been writing short stories and poetries since she was 6 years old. She manifested her views on life, emphasizing the enigmatic and arduous journey which are often thought provoking. Grace writes about nature, human emotions and divine love, using human love as an allegory. Grace is notorious for being a sleepyhead, most importantly a blithesome person. Her literary skills have gained recognition and have been awarded various awards.

Preface

"Cosmos In A Jar" invites you to embark on a journey through the labyrinth of emotions, thoughts, and perspectives that form the tapestry of human experience. Through the art of poetry, Grace Lalrinpari Hauzel seeks to capture the essence of moments, crystallizing them like stars in a cosmic jar. Each poem within this collection is a brushstroke on the canvas of existence, carefully composed to evoke feelings, provoke contemplation, and spark connections. As we read, we are invited to peer through the glass of our own perceptions, to discover the constellations of meaning that arise from the interplay of words and emotions.

With "Cosmos In A Jar," Grace crafts a symphony of language, weaving together threads of love, longing, introspection, and wonder. The cosmos, vast and unexplored, becomes a vessel for the complexities of the human heart and mind. As you turn these pages, let yourself be carried away on a journey that transcends time and space, guiding you through the labyrinthine corridors of imagination and understanding.

May these poems resonate with your own experiences, casting a soft glow on the intricacies of existence. Open this jar of cosmic verse and let its radiance illuminate the corners of your soul.

I Wish I May

I wish I may, I wish I might,
Upon a star, I dream tonight.
In the vast expanse of the midnight sky,
A longing stirs, as dreams go by.
I wish I may, I wish I might,
Find my way through the darkest night.
With every step, I strive to chase,
A path that leads to my destined place.
I wish I may, I wish I might,
Unleash the fire, ignite the light.
To make a change, to leave a mark,
To paint my dreams across the dark.
I wish I may, I wish I might,
Embrace the hope, hold it tight.
For in the whispers of my soul's plea,
Lies the promise of what could be.
I wish I may, I wish I might,
Shatter doubts, take flight.
Break free from chains that hold me down,
And rise, like wings upon the ground.
I wish I may, I wish I might,
Discover the strength, the will to fight.
To conquer fear, to conquer strife,
And construct a life I truly thrive.
I wish I may, I wish I might,

Find love's embrace, its gentle light.
To feel its warmth and tender touch,
As I journey through life's golden clutch.
I wish I may, I wish I might,
Savor each moment, day and night.
To taste the sweetness life has to offer,
And cherish every precious proffer.
I wish I may, I wish I might,
Always remember, never lose sight,
That dreams hold power, dreams hold sway,
And with belief, they pave the way.
So I close my eyes and make my plea,
To the universe, to set me free.
For in this wish, my heart reveals,
The dreams that guide, the love that heals.

Forever

Silent vows declared,
Two souls, endless in their love,
Forever intertwined.
Blossoms fade and fall,
Yet love's flame forever burns,
Timeless, pure and strong.
Infinite moments,
Eternity's embrace,
Love's forever dance.

Next To Nothing

In a world of constant hustle, where everything's in flight,
There's a beauty in the quiet, where shadows meet the light.
Next to nothing, yet it holds a world within,
A whispered tale of magic, where the journey will begin.
A single breath, a fleeting glance,
Next to nothing, but it's our chance.
To find the meaning in the spaces,
In the silence, find our places.
Next to nothing, we find it all,
In the stillness, we stand tall.
Uncover dreams that softly sing,
In the quiet, let our spirits take wing.
Beneath the stars that twinkle, in a midnight sky,
There's a symphony of secrets that only few may spy.
Next to nothing, yet the universe is there,
A canvas painted black, with wonders everywhere.
A distant echo, a gentle touch,
Next to nothing, it means so much.
To grasp the moments in their flight,
In the darkness, find our light.
In the rush and noise, we often miss,
The treasures found in a gentle kiss.
Next to nothing, a world unfolds,
In the stories that are silently told.
A whispered promise, a heart's embrace,

Next to nothing, a sacred space.
To hear the whispers of the soul,
In the hush, we find our role.

Firefly

Glowing in twilight,
Firefly dances with grace,
Nature's lantern light.
Tiny sparks of gold,
Whispering summer secrets,
Firefly's allure.
Night's starry canvas,
Firefly paints with its glow,
Nature's luminescence.

Break My Fall

A leap in the dark,
Your words so delicate,
Break my fall with grace.
A shattered heart's ache,
But your love's gentle embrace,
Breaks my fall, softly.
In moments of pain,
Your presence becomes my balm,
Break my fall and heal.

Breakdown

Under pressure's weight,
Mind succumbs to heavy load,
Cracks in sanity.
Thoughts scramble, chaotic,
Emotions ignite, ablaze,
Breakdown consumes all.
Fragile mind shatters,
Echoes of fragments scatter,
Seeking calm within.

Believe

Believe in your dreams,
Unwavering determination,
Success will follow.
In faith, find solace,
Believe in the unseen path,
Miracles will come.
Hold onto your hope,
Believe in infinite love,
Boundless joy awaits.

Rain

Rain falls from the sky
Cleansing the earth with its touch
Nature breaths and sighs
Pattering downpour
Leaves glisten with tiny gems
A symphony's start
Petrichor rises
Scent of wet earth fills the air
Life reborn, refreshed

Breath

Whispering through trees,
Nature's breath in gentle breeze,
Life alive, at ease.
Inhale, exhale slow,
Lungs fill with nature's pure flow,
Vitality shows.
Breath, essence of life,
In every moment, present,
Sustains, fuels, unites.

Evil Angel

Crimson wings expand,
Evil lurking in white feathers,
Deceptive angel.
Seductress in guise,
Halo tainted, soul corrupt,
Evil cherub smiles.
Innocence hidden,
Evil's touch, a fallen grace,
Dark angel in light.

Until The End

Rain falls softly down
Whispering secrets of time
Endless to the end
Sunset paints the sky
Splashing colors unending
Beauty till the end
Heart beats steadily
Love's eternal melody
Boundless, until end

Fade Away

With time's gentle touch,
Colors fade from vibrant hues,
Silent hues slip away.
Whispers on the wind,
Memories gently drifting,
Into the unknown.
Like morning dewdrops,
Ephemeral beauty fades,
Gone in the sunlight.

Crawl

Crawling through dim light,
Movement inches, a slow dance,
Strength found in small steps
Tiny legs explore,
Journey of discovery,
Crawling through life's tales
Underneath the earth,
Crawl the creatures, unseen world,
Nature's hidden realms

Hopeless

Twilight sky turns gray,
Hopeless dreams fade into mist,
Heart aches in silence.
Gloomy nights unfold,
Hopelessness engulfs my soul,
Searching for solace.
Flowers wither, bleak,
Hopeless whispers fill the air,
Lost within despair.

Into The Nothing

Into the nothing
Thoughts dissolve, fade away
Lost in empty void
Whispers dissipate
Silence engulfs every word
No echo returns
Endless abyss calls
Emptiness consumes the soul
Nothingness prevails

Lights Out

Silent darkness falls,
Lights extinguished one by one,
Whispers of shadows.
Inky veil descends,
A stillness hugs the dim night,
Lost in shadows' dance.
Glowing embers fade,
Shadows consume the moon's light,
Peace in darkness arms.

Without You

Whispers in the wind,
Empty spaces long for you,
Solace fades in me.
Silent nights linger,
Your absence aching my heart,
Yearning for your touch.
Blossoms bloom alone,
Your presence, the missing piece,
Incomplete without.

Failure

Dark clouds loom above,
Dreams tarnished, plans shattered wide,
Failure's bitter taste.
A broken path, lost,
Lessons learned through stumbles hard,
Failure builds strength.
Failure's icy touch,
Yet within, seeds of success,
Blossoms from ashes.

Angels Fall

Angels in free flight,
Feathers gently touch the ground,
Graceful in their fall.
Wings once white as snow,
Now tarnished, with flaws to show,
Angels stumble low.
Descending in fate,
Angels seek redemption's gate,
Finding peace, innate.

Breaking The Silence

Breaking the silence,
Words flow like a gentle breeze,
Healing hearts anew.
Whispers shatter walls,
Truth lingers within the air,
Silence no more.
Embrace the courage,
Speak, for your voice has power,
Silence shall crumble.

Close To Heaven

Golden rays break through
Crown of mountains touch the sky
Close to heaven's reach
In the mist and clouds
Whispering winds brush my face
Close to heaven's grace
Eyes cast to the peak
Where dreams and heavens collide
Close to heaven's door

Never Again

Aching hearts vow strong,
Never again we shall falter,
Seeking peace's song.
Scattered memories,
Never again to endure,
Healing starts to bloom.
Whispers of anguish,
Never again shall we bear,
Love's light shall prevail.

The Great Divide

A canyon so deep,
Separates us, love and hate,
Bridging hearts takes time.
Mountains of discord,
Divide souls on different paths,
Seek unity's peak.
Chasms wide and vast,
Bridging hope and understanding,
Humanity's choice.

Psycho

Madness deep within,
Psycho's twisted, dark desires,
Mind's chaos unleashed.
A psychopath's waltz,
In a twisted dance of death,
Eyes devoid of warmth.
Fractured sanity,
Psycho's soul in disarray,
Horror's masterpiece.

The Dark Of You

Shrouded silence falls,
In the void of your absence,
Whispers in shadows.
Moonbeams softly weep,
As your darkness engulfs me,
Lost in your abyss.
Love's secrets unfold,
In depths of your mystic soul,
Entwined, forever.

Torn In Two

Heart caught in a storm,
Torn in two, a soul divides,
Seeking calm's embrace.
Silent battlefield,
Love's battle waged in whispers,
Torn hearts bleed in hush.
In two worlds they dwell,
Yearning whispers fill the void,
Aching souls torn wide.

Save Yourself

Save yourself, dear soul,
Find strength in your own being,
Rescue from within.
Amidst chaos, thrive,
Seek solace in self-care's art,
Healing, like a balm.
Embrace your story,
In your refuge, reinvent,
Marvelscape of YOU.

Close Your Eyes

Close your eyes and dream,
Whispering wind brings solace,
Peace in darkness gleams.
In silence, the world
unveils its hidden wonders,
see with mind unfurled.
Behind your closed eyes,
a universe awaits you,
where dreams touch the skies.

Promise Blender

Stainless machine spins,
Blending hopes and dreams to one,
Promise in a cup.
Whirling like the wind,
Promises blend together,
In a trusty bond.
With blades of pure hope,
A blender of promises,
Deliver one's word.

Safe With You

In your warm embrace
Secure, protected, I find
Trust blossoms like spring
Within your haven
Every worry fades away
Love shelters my soul
Together we stand
A fortress against the storm
Safe in love's embrace

Boundaries

Limitations set,
Creating space for growth,
Boundaries define.
A line in the sand,
Separating what's within,
And what lies beyond.
Edges of our world,
Marking where we end and start,
Boundaries of life.

Locked In A Cage

Locked in a cold cage,
Yearning for freedom's warm touch,
Wings clipped, dreams caged tight.
Steel bars confine me,
Silent screams echo within,
Yearning for release.
Caged spirit, confined,
But hope lingers deep inside,
Freedom's key awaits.

More Faithful

True love never wanes
Through storms, it stands unyielding
Faithful hearts endure
Loyal till the end
A bond that cannot be bent
Trust, the foundation
In fidelity
Promises intertwined souls
Forever faithful

Suspended In You

Suspended in time,
Within your poetic world,
Words dance in my heart.
In your gentle touch,
Emotions vividly paint,
Whispering their truth.

Whirlwind

In swirling chaos,
Leaves take flight, dance in the wind,
Nature's wild embrace.
Unseen force of air,
Spiraling in a frenzy,
Whirlwind stirs the soul.
Cyclone of passion,
Hearts entwined in twirling bliss,
Love's whirlwind prevails.

The One

In boundless starry skies,
Our souls once lost, now entwined,
Love's light forever.
Whisper of your name,
Echoes intertwine in time,
Destiny's embrace.
Across dimensions,
A lone soul, two hearts aligned,
One flame eternally.

You're In My Brain

Thinking, processing,
Neurons spark, thoughts alight,
Mind's infinite depth.
Hidden labyrinth,
Neurons weave, mapping knowledge,
Brain's sublime fortress.
In dreams, neurons dance,
Imaginary realms bloom,
Thoughts wander freely.

You're My Hope

From darkest despair,
Blooms a flower of hope bright,
Guiding steps to light.
Morning's golden rays,
Whispering promises true,
Hope births in my heart.
Storms may rage and howl,
But fragile ember within,
Kindles hope, anew.

Will You Be There?

Lost in darkest night
Will you be there by my side?
Guiding me to light.
Through trials we face
Strength in your presence I find
Will you be there, love?
In joy and sorrow
Together, through thick and thin
Will you be there, friend?

Come My Way

Come my way, dear love
Through the fields of golden dreams
Our souls intertwine
In whispered moments
Time slows down, a gentle breeze
Guides us, hand in hand
Under moonlit skies
Our hearts dance, eternally
Love's melody plays

Forsaken

Memories fade fast,
Long lost dreams, forsaken hopes,
Whisper in the wind.
Empty promises,
Forsaken love, shattered trust,
Heartache's bitter taste.
Abandoned and lone,
Forsaken soul seeks solace,
Nature's arms embrace.

Open Wounds

Shattered hearts bleed pain,
Open wounds, whispers of loss,
Healing takes its time.
Fragile skin breaks, tears,
Beneath scars, stories unfold,
Surviving battles.
Crimson rivers flow,
Open wounds embrace healing,
Strength grows from within.

Collide

Autumn leaves whisper,
Their unique hues intertwined,
Nature's dance divine.
Two souls, lost in time,
Fate brings them together, bound,
Love's collision found.
Worlds converge, collide,
Ideas clash, sparks ignite,
Creativity.

Imperfection

Imperfect petals,
Beauty in their delicate flaws,
Nature's unique art.
Crooked lines reveal
The authentic hand of time,
Imperfection shines.
Incomplete puzzle,
Missing piece completes the whole,
Perfect imperfection.

Under My Skin

Whispers on my flesh,
Intricate patterns unfold,
Under my skin, art.
Ink etched deep within,
Stories hidden, tales untold,
Under my skin, life.
Invisible lines trace,
Emotions buried embrace,
Under my skin, grace.

Rebirth

Born from ashes, anew,
Phoenix spreads its fiery wings,
Rebirth ignites life.
Silent winter's grip,
Blossoms awaken with spring,
Nature's rebirth song.
Serpents shed old skin,
Emerging with vibrant scales,
Renewal's embrace.

Yours To Hold

Whispers of your touch,
Comfort, warmth within my grasp,
Love, forever kept.
In timeless embrace,
Yours to hold, a precious gift,
Souls entwined, complete.
Fragile, like a dream,
Yet sturdy in faithful hands,
Love's treasure, I'll keep.

Monster

Monstrous and fierce,
Eyes glowing with darkness deep,
Nightmare's haunting sleep.
A creature lurking,
Underneath the moonlit trees,
Fear its growling sound.
In shadows it hides,
Monstrously, it waits to strike,
Heart trembling with fright.

May Be Memories

Faded photographs,
Whispers of forgotten times,
Memories remain.
Dancing in my mind,
Melting sunsets, gentle breeze,
Nostalgic embrace.
Footprints on the sand,
Echoes of laughter and love,
Preserved in my heart.

Poetic Tragedy

Ink runs down the page,
Words lost in tragic downfall,
Poetry weeps.
Melancholic verse,
Heartache etched in every line,
Tragedy's sweet song.
Words dance like ashes,
Haunting whispers of sorrow,
Poetic tragedy.

Blue And Yellow

Blue sky stretches wide
Yellow sun shines so brightly
Nature's perfect blend
Bluebird takes to flight
Yellow flowers bloom below
Nature's harmony
Blue ocean meets sand
Yellow sunset paints the sky
Beauty intertwined

On My Own

Walking the empty
streets, thoughts echo loudly -
solitude whispers.
Alone with my thoughts,
I wander, lost in my mind,
finding myself there.
Silent footsteps tread,
freedom found in solitude,
discovering me.

Pieces Mended

Broken hearts, shattered
Fragments woven together
Love's tapestry formed
Scattered dreams take flight
Once shattered, now whole again
Hope's whispers arise
Mending shattered bonds
Resilience in each stitch
Unity restored

Take It Away

A voice, soft and pure
Melodies dancing on air
Take it away, love
Fingers strumming strings
Music's gentle lullaby
Take it away, peace
Heartache fades away
Lyrics cleanse a troubled soul
Take it away, pain

All That I've Got

Lost in your love's depth
Unveiling unknown desires
All that I've got, you
Whispers in moonlight
Serenading our spirits
All that I've got, love
Heart's canvas painted
With every beat, devotion
All that I've got, true

Hard To Say

Words held on my tongue
Difficult to find their way
Silently they fade
Thoughts tangled and frayed
Speech halts, stumbles on each sound
Hard to say, I try
Whispers of secret
Hidden meanings, unspoken
A language unseen

Find A Way

Through misty valleys,
Paths emerge for those who seek,
Find a way, don't yield.
Peaks beyond reach seem,
But hope echoes through the wind,
Find a way, persist.
Lost in the darkness,
Stars guide us to brighter days,
Find a way, ignite.

Empty With You

Silent solitude,
Embracing emptiness's gift,
Together, we thrive.
Empty spaces speak,
Whispering their gentle truth,
You complete my soul.
In your presence, dear,
Hollowness transforms into,
A sacred union.

On The Cross

On the cross he hung,
Suffering for all our sins,
Love's ultimate gift.
Pain pierced through his flesh,
Redemption in his last breath,
Hope blooms from his wounds.
His sacrifice pure,
Death defeated, life restored,
Grace whispers through time.

Come Undone

Tangled in heartache,
Fragile threads unraveling,
Love's masterpiece fades.
Once bound together,
Whispered promises now lost,
Fractured souls collide.
Shattered like glass, we
Watch our love's fragments scatter,
Yet hope remains small.

Meant To Die

Crimson leaves falling,
Life's beauty fading away,
Nature bids farewell.
Whispers of autumn,
A fragile dance with demise,
Serenade in death.
Silent cries echo,
Embracing the fleeting breath,
Existence undone.

The Best Of Me

Unseen depths unfold,
In moments of purest grace,
The best of me shines.
Beneath shadows, bright,
Emerges strength and wisdom,
My essence revealed.
Through trials endured,
Blossoms resilience and hope,
The best of me blooms.

For You

I breathe love for you,
Words cascade from my heart's depths,
In this humble verse.
Each syllable traced,
Paints a portrait of my soul,
Expressing my love.
For you, this poem,
A token of my truest,
Everlasting love.

Broken Windows

Broken glass shattered,
Windows once held light and hope,
Now darkness remains.
Cracks spider their way,
Across fragile panes of glass,
Fractured memories.
Windows once framed dreams,
Now lay shattered on the ground,
Hope will be rebuilt.

The Divine Absence

Seeking the divine,
Silent void, absence of God,
Mystery unfolds.
Empty sanctuary,
Whispers of spirits now gone,
Faith in solitude.
Divine absence, deep,
Yearning hearts, searching for signs,
In cosmic stillness.

Over And Over Again

Over and again,
Echoes of the past resound,
Time loops, never ends.
Repetition's song,
Moments on an endless loop,
Patterns woven deep.
Cycles intertwine,
A dance of eternal return,
Life's relentless spin.

The Quiet War

Whispers in the night
Shadows dance in silent steps
Conflict cloaked in hush
Words hold their power
Beneath layers of tension
Silence fuels the fight
A battlefield still
Unspoken battles waged deep
Peace lost in mere breath

The Ransom

Confinement ensues,
Twisted realm of desperation,
Fragments of life lost.
Demands shouted loud,
Priceless value, freedom held,
Fate sealed, hope evades.
A heart's heavy weight,
Ransom paid, shackles broken,
Victory, freedom.

As You're Falling Down

Autumn leaves descend,
Whispering fate's gentle touch,
Gravity's embrace.
Fragile hearts collide,
In the midst of wings now lost,
Boundless freedom fades.
Time slows, senses reel,
In this descent, a love blooms,
Fluidity found.

Reverse This Curse

Reverse the dark curse,
With love's light, it shall disperse,
Hope will then immerse.
Lost in shadows deep,
Seeking solace, I entreat,
Curse's end I keep.
Whispers of despair,
Breaking free from lifelong snare,
Curse reversed, repair.

My Apocalypse

In darkness I dwell,
Worlds collapse and chaos reigns,
My soul finds solace.
Fire engulfs all life,
Ashes whisper of the past,
Apocalypse thrives.
Silent desolation,
My universe crumbles down,
Hope rises anew.

You're So Beautiful

Radiant delight
Your smile embraces my heart
Beauty like no other
In your gentle gaze
I find solace and comfort
A love beyond words
Graceful and serene
Each feature a masterpiece
You're an angel, dear

Perfect Nightmare

Darkness wraps around
Nightmares whisper in my ear
Perfection in fear
Twisted, haunting dreams
Perfect nightmare takes control
Sleep's sweet agony
Silent screams echo
Perfect nightmare's icy grip
Awake, yet trapped still

World Around Me

Morning sun rises,
Nature awakens with grace,
World breathes in new life.
City streets bustling,
People lost in their own worlds,
Amidst concrete dreams.
Mountains kiss the sky,
Rivers flow towards the sea,
World's beauty unfolds.

Painting

There goes the sun's light,
Painting hues across the sky,
Day whispers goodbye.
Embracing twilight,
Silent symphony unfolds,
Sun's final adieu.
Golden glow recedes,
Horizon swallows the sun,
Night's reign now begins.

Life In Light

A sunbeam whispers,
Embracing the darkest nights,
Life glows from within.
Shadows dance and fade,
In rays of hope, we find strength,
Light guides our footsteps.
Golden hues reveal,
The beauty that lies within,
Life's intricate art.

Kick The Bucket

A life fades away,
Bucket kicked, journey complete,
Memories remain.
Moments cherished, gone,
Bucket kicked, now at peace,
Whispers in the wind.
Bucket empty, full,
Life's fragility revealed,
Footprints etched in time.

Afterlife

Eternal darkness,
Souls find solace, peace, release,
Beyond the mortal realm.
Transcendent beauty,
Unseen realms, ethereal light,
Afterlife's embrace.
Mysteries unveiled,
In the afterlife's refuge,
Soul's eternal quest.

The Greatest Story

He's risen again,
Death defeated, hope returns,
Resurrection's light.
From the grave emerges,
Life's triumph over darkness,
Rejoice in his name.
Wounds healed, love prevails,
New life springs from eternal,
Faith in resurrection.